What Now?

.

WHAT NOW?

A Bible Study for Growing Believers

Teacher Edition

John Thomas Clark, Thm, DMin

Tetelestai Press

ISBN: 978-1-7353359-0-2

CONTENTS

ACKNOWLEDGEMENTS

"What Now" was born out of a desire to provide a helpful tool for disciple-makers. While engaged in personal evangelism, it became evident that I needed a tool to walk a new believer through the most basic and essential elements of their new Christian life. I began to search for such a tool on the internet, and although I found many helpful books, none of them had the interactive, replicable type of study I was looking for. Hence the birth of "What Now?"

The concept of a fill-in-the-blank study comes from my exposure to this method through a mission organization (Disciple Makers Multiplied – www.dm2usa.org) led by one of my mentors, Bret Nazworth. This method has been a helpful tool in equipping disciple-makers all around the world.

The actual content of the booklet is a combination of the author's own teaching along with heavy reliance upon two other booklets designed for new believers. Those two booklets are "I'm Saved! Now What?" by Dennis M. Rokser (which you can find on Amazon - https://www.amazon.com/Saved-Now-What-Dennis-Rokser/dp/1939110017 OR at Grace Gospel Press - https://www.gracegospelpress.org/im-saved-now-what/) AND "Welcome to the Family" by R. Larry Moyer (which you can find on Amazon - https://www.amazon.com/Welcome-Family-Understanding-Relationship-Othersebook/dp/B07PXNPMG2).

Again, my desire was NOT just to duplicate tools that were already in the market place, but rather provide a study that could enable someone to meet in a one-on-one or a small group interactive setting with booklets, and fill-in-the-blank materials. I am praying this booklet will be used by God, according to His desire, to ground and establish new believers in the faith and to put them also on the road to future disciple-making endeavors of their own!

By His Grace,
John Thomas Clark, Thm, DMin

WHAT NOW?—REVIEW OF SALVATION

A QUICK (but important) REVIEW

If you have trusted in Jesus Christ as your personal Savior, you have been born again by God's grace. You have entered the spiritual family of God! Welcome to the forgiven and forever family of God. As you have come to understand through the Scriptures (a.k.a. the Bible), the first issue between you and God was **NOT** a change in your ___**behavior**___, as needed as that might be. Instead it was an issue of spiritual birth and a change in your eternal destiny, being born again into the family of God and being guaranteed a home in Heaven. When you believed that Jesus Christ is God who became a man and died for your sins and rose from the dead to give you eternal life as a ___**free**___ ___**gift**___, many things became true of you. We will detail these things throughout this study, but first…a review.

John 3:16 encapsulates the main message of the Bible and so let us take a moment to review it. The verse itself could be broken down into four separate parts: (1) The context, (2) The content, (3) The response, and (4) The result. John 3:16 reads:

1

> *"For God so loved the world*
> *that He gave His only begotten Son,*
> *that whoever believes in Him*
> *should not perish but have everlasting life."*

The Context: "For God"

Holy—Since John 3:16 starts off with God, a person must know who God is in His character to understand the verse. The Bible teaches us that God is **holy**, righteous, and just in His character (Psalm 99:9). This means that God is perfect or pure, and of necessity without sin. For us to correctly grasp God's holy character, He gave the **law**, which contains His commandments. These include commandments to not commit murder, adultery, theft, bearing false witness against one's neighbor (i.e. lying), or coveting. If we break even one of these commandments, just once (James 2:10), we have **sinned** and are considered sinners and guilty before God (Romans 3:23).

Just—The Bible also describes God as being Just, which means that He is **fair**, that He punishes wrongdoers and He gives people what they deserve. There is a penalty for breaking God's law, and because God is just, He must execute the **penalty** on lawbreakers. The penalty is described in Romans 6:23a as death. Death in the Bible never means nonexistence, but rather separation, like the soul and spirit of a man being separated from his body at the point of physical death. This means that mankind has **earned** or deserved his spiritual "wages" of death (or separation from God for eternity).

Summary—Because God is holy and just in His character, and because mankind is not as evidenced by their inability to keep God's holy standards, mankind faces a "death" penalty which includes separation from God for eternity. If God were to give mankind what they deserved (because He is just), everyone one would __**deserve**__ hell.

The Content: "so loved the world that He gave His only begotten Son"

No amount of good works or religious rituals could ever save you from a Hell you deserve to a Heaven you do not deserve, since good works do not __**pay**__ the death penalty. Additionally, we read in Isaiah 64:6 that "all our righteousnesses are as filthy rags." Notice it says our *righteousnesses* and NOT our *UN-righteousnesses*. The absolute best we have to offer to God in terms of our own holiness is filthy menstrual rags[1].

This is why the good news of the gospel states that God so loved the world that He gave His only begotten Son to die to pay the __**penalty**__ for the sins of all mankind that the holiness and justice of God *required*. Romans 5:8 says, "But God demonstrates His own love toward us, in that while we were still sinners, Christ *died* **for us.**" What was the penalty for our sin? Death (Romans 6:23a). What did Christ do for us? He died for us, paying the very penalty hanging over our head.

The good news of the Gospel states that Jesus Christ "died for our sins according to the Scriptures, and that He was buried, and that He rose again the third day according to the Scriptures" (1 Corinthians 15:3-4). When Jesus died on the cross, His last words were "It Is Finished," indicating that your sins were paid in full forever, and the fact that God raised Him from the dead indicates that God __**accepts**__ Jesus Christ's substitutionary death on your behalf.

Summary—God sent Jesus Christ to earth to die a __ **substitutionary**__ death, paying the penalty for our sins, so that we would not have to face the death penalty and so that we could be saved from a Hell that we deserved.

The Response: "that whoever believes in Him"

God's gift of eternal salvation has become personally yours the very moment you transferred your faith from a church that cannot save you, or a ritual that cannot forgive you, or attempts at a holy life which could never redeem you, and instead you placed your __**faith**__ in the Lord Jesus Christ. Why Jesus? Because He is the One who died for you, paying your penalty, and He rose again, showing us God accepted His payment on your behalf.

Many people confuse the biblical response to the Gospel in our day. You may have heard the following: "Give your heart (or life) to Christ," "You must walk the aisle," "You need to pray the 'sinner's prayer,'" "You need to commit your heart (or life) to Christ," "You must ask Jesus into your heart," "You must be baptized," "You must publicly confess Christ to others," "You need to ask God for forgiveness of your sins." Would it surprise you to find that ___***NONE***___ of these responses are ever given in the Bible as the response mankind needs to have in order to be __**saved**__? The Bible is very clear…"believe on the Lord Jesus Christ and you will be saved" (Acts 16:31).

Ephesians 2:8-9 says this, "For by grace you have been saved through *faith*, and that *not of yourselves*; it is the gift of God, *not of works*, lest anyone should boast."

Summary—Jesus Christ completely paid the penalty for our sins, and so there is nothing left for us to do but to simply _____**trust**_____ in Him that He did indeed do what He says He did. We must put our faith in the One who died for us.

The Result: "should not perish but have eternal life."

According to John 3:16, the result of believing in Jesus Christ as your Savior is that you will never have to face the death _____**penalty**_____ (i.e. *should not perish*) and you now possess eternal life. Eternal life, by definition, goes on forever and **never** ends. How could God guarantee such great results without first watching how a person will respond to His free gift? Shouldn't God put people on somewhat of a probation period before He makes such extreme promises?

God can guarantee these two results, because they rest solely upon Jesus Christ's _____**finished**_____ work and faithfulness rather than your own insufficient works. If you could still perish or if eternal life could be taken away from you as a result of sin in your life or insufficient good works, then Christ's promise here would not be true. Additionally, if a maintenance of good works were necessary to procure or secure eternal life, then it could not be called a "_____**gift**_____" as it is in Romans 6:23b, "...but the gift of God is eternal life in Christ Jesus our Lord."

Summary—When a person puts their faith in Jesus Christ,

5

God makes two promises in John 3:16: (1) That person will not perish, meaning they will never face the death penalty due them as a result of their sin, and (2) They now possess eternal life, which by definition lasts forever.

In Conclusion

The million dollar question is this: "Will you or have you put your faith in Jesus Christ __**alone**__, that He died for your sins, in your place, and that He rose again on the third day, showing us that God accepted His sacrifice as a substitute in your place?"

If not, what is holding you back from putting your faith in Jesus Christ alone?

If so, why don't you stop right now and __**thank**__ God for providing eternal salvation to you as a free gift? Why not thank Jesus Christ for having loved you by dying on the cross for your sins and rising from the dead to personally give you eternal life apart from your works?

WHAT NOW?—SPIRITUAL BLESSINGS IN CHRIST

INTRODUCTION

Unbeknownst to most people who have recently put their faith in Jesus Christ alone, they now possess many spiritual blessings. In fact, there are at least __215__ things that are true of you now that you are saved! We will spend time in this study to review some of these glorious truths about who you are now "**IN** Christ."

The Truth of the Matter

2 Corinthians 5:17 says this, "Therefore, if anyone *is **in*** Christ, *he is* a new creation; old things have passed away; behold, all things have become new." God states emphatically that you have become a new creation "**IN** Christ." But let us clarify something immediately lest you be confused from the onset. When 2 Corinthians 5:17 says, "old things have passed away; behold, all things have become new," it is not teaching that all of your sinful practices have now __ceased__. Nor is it stating that all your wrong thoughts and beliefs have instantaneously __changed__ (I wish this were true, but it is not). Instead

these issues of your daily Christian living will only be addressed and changed through the ongoing process of spiritual growth as you repeatedly study and receive the Word of God by faith and ___**apply**___ it in your life. The new creation spoken of refers to the believer's new ___**indentity**___ in Jesus Christ, and not their behavior.

In relation to our new "identity" in Christ, the Bible says that God views all of mankind in one of ___**two**___ groups: (1) Those who are **IN** Adam, and (2) Those who are **IN** Christ. Let us read Romans 5:12-21 and see the differences between those two positions.

IN ADAM Before Salvation		IN CHRIST After Salvation
Dead in Sin		Regenerated/Made Alive
Unrighteous		Justified—Declared Righteous
No Peace	✝	Peace with God/Peace of God
No Access		Full and Unlimited Access
No Hope		Hope
Ungodly		Accepted in Christ
Sinners		Saints
Under Divine Wrath		Saved from Wrath
Enemies of God		Reconciled to God
Lost		Saved

Ephesians 1:3 says, "Blessed *be* the God and Father of our Lord Jesus Christ, who has blessed us with *__every__* spiritual blessing in the heavenly *places* in Christ." It is helpful to observe that every believer in Christ (not just ___**some**___) has already

been blessed (as a ___**past**___ reality) with every spiritual blessing (not every physical one) in the heavenly places (the believer's new realm of existence) in Christ (because of their identity or ___**union**___ with Christ). What are some of the spiritual blessings that you now have "in Christ?" Consider the following partial list[1] of what is yours and every believer's in Christ. Based upon the authority of God's Word:

1. My salvation is fully accomplished (John 19:30).
2. I have eternal life as a present possession (John 5:24; 6:47; 1 John 5:11-13).
3. I have Jesus Christ as my present possession (1 John 5:12).
4. I know the one, true God (John 17:3; 1 John 2:3; 5:20).
5. I have been saved by His grace (Eph. 2:1-10).
6. I have been justified by His grace (Tit. 3:7).
7. I have passed from death unto life (John 5:24; 1 John 3:14).
8. I have been quickened (made alive) by God (Eph. 2:1,5; Col. 2:13).
9. I have been made fit for heaven (Col. 1:12).
10. I have the forgiveness of sins (Eph. 1:7; Col. 1:14).
11. My sins have been taken away (John 1:29; Heb. 9:26; 1 John 3:5).
12. My sins have been completely purged (Heb. 1:3).
13. My sins will never be remembered by God (Heb. 8:12; 10:17).
14. I have been washed (1 Cor. 6:11; Tit. 3:5; Rev. 1:5).
15. I will walk with Christ in white (Rev. 3:4-5).
16. I have been healed by His stripes (1 Pet. 2:24).
17. I have been forgiven all trespasses (Col. 2:13; 1 John

9

2:12).

18. I have been fully justified (Rom. 4:5; 8:30; 1 Cor. 6:11; Gal. 2:16; Tit. 3:7).

19. I am reconciled to God (2 Cor. 5:18-19; Col. 1:20).

20. I am made nigh by the blood of Christ (Eph. 2:13).

21. I am redeemed through His blood (1 Pet. 1:18,19; Eph. 1:7; Col. 1:14).

22. I am redeemed from the curse of the law (Gal. 3:13).

23. I am redeemed from all iniquity or lawlessness (Titus 2:14).

24. I am bought with a price (1 Cor. 6:20; 7:23).

25. I am delivered from so great a death (2 Cor. 1:10).

26. I have been delivered from this present evil world or age (Gal. 1:4).

27. I have been delivered from the power of darkness (Col. 1:13).

28. I have been delivered from the wrath to come (1 Thess. 1:10).

29. I will not come into condemnation or judgment (John 5:24; Rom. 8:1).

30. I am a child of God (John 1:12; Rom. 8:16; Gal. 3:26; 1 John 3:1,2).

31. I am a son of God (Gal. 4:5-7).

32. I belong to Jesus Christ (Gal. 3:29; 5:24).

33. I have been adopted (Gal. 4:5; Rom. 8:15,23).

34. I am an heir of God and joint-heir with Christ (Rom. 8:17; Tit. 3:7).

35. I am an heir of the grace of life (1 Pet. 3:7).

36. All things are mine (1 Cor. 3:21-23).

37. I possess all things (2 Cor. 6:10).

38. I will inherit all things (Rev. 21:7).

39. I am enriched by Christ in everything (1 Cor. 1:5; 2 Cor. 9:11).

40. I am a fellow heir (Eph. 3:6).

41. I am rich because of Christ (2 Cor. 8:9; Rev. 2:9).

42. I am blessed with every spiritual blessing (Eph. 1:3).

43. I have obtained an inheritance (Eph. 1:11,14; Heb. 1:14; 9:15; 1 Pet. 1:4).

44. I have been appointed to obtain salvation (1 Thess. 5:9; Heb. 1:14).

45. I am His inheritance (Eph. 1:18).

46. I am a partaker of His promise in Christ by the gospel (Eph. 3:6).

47. I am a new creature (creation) in Christ (2 Cor. 5:17; Eph. 2:10; 4:24; Col. 3:10).

48. I have been renewed by the Holy Spirit (Tit. 3:5).

49. I am accepted and highly favored in the Beloved One (Eph. 1:6; cf. Matt. 3:17).

50. I have been seated in heavenly places with Christ (Eph. 2:6).

51. I am to the praise of His glory (Eph. 1:6,12).

52. I am light in the Lord (Eph. 5:8).

53. I am a child of light (Eph. 5:8; 1 Thess. 5:5).

54. I am a "peculiar person," even God's special, purchased possession (Tit. 2:14; 1 Pet.2:9).

55. I am a priest who can offer spiritual sacrifices (Heb. 13:15-16; 1 Pet. 2:5,9; Rev. 1:6; 5:10;20:6).

56. I am a king who will reign (Rev. 1:6; 5:10; 20:6).

57. I am privileged to have fellowship with the Father and with the Son (1 John 1:3).

58. I dwell in Christ (John 6:56; 1 John 3:24; 4:13,15,16).

59. Christ dwells in me (John 6:56; Gal. 2:20; 1 John 3:24;

4:12-16).

60. I am in Christ (John 14:20; 2 Cor. 5:17).

61. Christ is in me (John 14:20; Col. 1:27; Rom. 8:10; 1 John 4:4).62. The Spirit of God dwells in me (Rom. 8:9; 1 Cor. 3:16; Eph. 2:21-22).

62. The Spirit of God dwells (John 6:56; Gal. 2:20; 1 John 3:24; 4:12-16).

63. I am not in the flesh but in the Spirit (Rom. 8:9).

64. My "earthen vessel" houses a great Treasure (2 Cor. 4:7).

65. My body is the temple of the Holy Spirit (1 Cor. 6:19).

66. I have been blessed with the gift and pledge of the Holy Spirit (2 Cor. 1:22; Gal. 4:6; Eph. 1:13-14; 1 Thess. 4:8; Tit. 3:6; 1 John 3:24; 4:13).

67. I have an anointing (unction) from the Holy One (1 John 2:20,27).

68. I am one of the "called" of Jesus Christ (Rom. 1:6; 8:28-30; Jude 1; Rev. 17:14).

69. I have been called unto the fellowship of God's Son (1 Cor. 1:9).

70. I have been called unto eternal glory (1 Pet. 5:10).

71. I have been called with a holy calling (2 Tim. 1:9).

72. I am a partaker of the high, heavenly calling (Phil. 3:14; Heb. 3:1).

73. I have been called out of darkness into His marvelous light (1 Pet. 2:9).

74. God foreknew me (Rom. 8:29; 1 Pet. 1:2).

75. God predestined me to be conformed to Christ's image (Rom. 8:29; Eph. 1:5,11).

76. I have already been glorified according to God's mind and purpose (Rom. 8:30).

77. I am eternally secure in God's love (Rom. 8:38-39).

78. I am chosen in Christ (Eph. 1:4; Col. 3:12; 1 Thess. 1:4; 1 Pet. 2:9; Rev. 17:14).

79. I have been chosen to salvation (2 Thess. 2:13).

80. I am complete in Christ (Col. 2:10).

81. I am beloved of God (Col. 3:12; 2 Thess. 2:13).

82. I am chastened and disciplined by my Heavenly Father (Heb. 12:6-7).

83. I am part of that group that Christ is not ashamed to call His "brethren" and "friends" (Heb. 2:11; John 15:14-15).

84. I am a child of Abraham (Gal. 3:7).

85. I am Abraham's seed (Gal. 3:29).

86. I enjoy the blessing of Abraham (Gal. 3:9).

87. I am a child of promise (Gal. 4:28,31).

88. I am faithful (Rev. 17:14).

89. I am a sheep in His flock (Luke 12:32; Heb. 13:20; 1 Pet. 2:25).

90. I am a member of His body (1 Cor. 10:17; 12:27; Eph. 3:6; 4:25; 5:30).

91. I am a stone in His building (Eph. 2:20-22; Heb. 3:6; 1 Pet. 2:5).

92. I am a branch in the Vine (John 15:1-7).

93. I am a child of the kingdom (Matt. 13:38; compare Mark 10:14-15).

94. I am born again into His family (John 1:12-13; James 1:18; 1 Pet. 1:3,23; 2:2; 1 John 5:1).

95. I am one of God's people because He graciously claims me as His own (1 Pet. 2:10; Rev. 21:7).

96. I am a fellow citizen with the saints (Eph. 2:19).

97. I was baptized into Jesus Christ (Rom. 6:3; Gal. 3:27).

98. I was identified with Christ in His death (Rom. 6:3-6,8-11; 2 Cor. 5:14; Col. 2:12,20; 3:3).

99. I was identified with Christ in His resurrection (Rom. 6:5,8,11; 2 Cor. 5:15; Gal. 2:20; Col. 2:12; 3:1).

100. I died to sin (Rom. 6:2).

101. My "old man" was crucified with Christ (Rom. 6:6).

102. I have been crucified with Christ (Gal. 2:20).

103. I have crucified the flesh with its affections and lusts (Gal. 5:24).

104. I am alive unto God (Rom. 6:11,13; Gal. 2:19,20).

105. Christ is my life (Phil. 1:21; Col. 3:4).

106. I can walk in newness of life (Rom. 6:4).

107. I can serve in newness of spirit (Rom. 7:6).

108. I can live unto righteousness (1 Pet. 2:24).

109. I died to the law (Rom. 7:4; Gal. 2:19).

110. I am delivered from the law (Rom. 7:6).

111. I am not under the law but under grace (Rom. 6:14).

112. I have God's laws written in my heart (Heb. 10:16).

113. I am married to Jesus Christ (Rom. 7:4).

114. I am a partaker of Christ (Heb. 3:14).

115. I am identified with Christ in His suffering (2 Tim. 2:12; Phil. 1:29; 1 Pet. 2:20; 4:12-13; 1 Thess. 3:3; Rom. 8:18; Col. 1:24).

116. The knowledge of God is made known by me (2 Cor. 2:14).

117. The savor (aroma) of Christ is made known by me (2 Cor. 2:15-16).

118. I am an epistle of Christ (2 Cor. 3:3).

119. I am being changed into Christ's glorious image (2 Cor. 3:18).

120. I am being perfected (Phil. 1:6).

121. My inward man is being renewed day by day (2 Cor. 4:16).

122. I have put on Christ (Gal. 3:27).

123. I am not of the world (John 17:14,16).

124. The world is crucified unto me (Gal. 6:14).

125. I am crucified unto the world (Gal. 6:14).

126. I am separated unto the gospel of God (Rom. 1:1).

127. I am set apart and sanctified in Christ Jesus (1 Cor. 1:2; 6:11; Heb. 10:10; Jude 1).

128. I am holy (Col. 3:12; Heb. 3:1; 1 Pet. 2:9; Rev. 20:6).

129. I am clothed in His righteousness (Rev. 19:8).

130. I am a saint (1 Cor. 1:2; Phil. 1:1; Col. 1:2; Rom. 1:7).

131. I am faultless in Christ (Eph. 5:27; Col. 1:22; Jude 24).

132. I am perfected forever (Heb. 10:14).

133. I am not my own (1 Cor. 6:19).

134. I am called unto holiness (1 Thess. 4:7).

135. I am a citizen of heaven (Phil. 3:20).

136. I am a stranger and pilgrim who is not at home in this world (Heb. 11:13; 1 Pet. 2:11).

137. I have been translated into the kingdom of the Son of His love (Col. 1:13).

138. I am circumcised in my heart (Col. 2:11; Phil 3:3; compare Deut. 10:16).

139. My faithful God will sanctify me wholly (1 Thess. 5:23-24).

140. My faithful God will keep me from evil (2 Thess. 3:3; 2 Tim. 4:18).

141. Christ has made me free, free indeed (John 8:32-36; Gal. 5:1; 1 Cor. 7:22).

142. Jesus Christ is my Deliverer (Rom. 7:24-25).

143. I am free from sin (Rom. 6:7,18,22).

144. The law of the Spirit of Life has made me free from the law of sin and death (Rom. 8:2).

145. I am God's servant or slave (Rom. 6:22).

146. I am Christ's servant or slave (1 Cor. 7:22).

147. I am a servant or slave of righteousness (Rom. 6:18).

148. I have been called unto liberty (Gal. 5:13).

149. I have the mind of Christ (1 Cor. 2:16).

150. I have a sound mind (2 Tim. 1:7).

151. Christ has given me an understanding (1 John 5:20).

152. I have the righteousness of Christ (2 Cor. 5:21).

153. I have all sufficiency in all things (2 Cor. 9:8).

154. I have all things that pertain to life and godliness (2 Pet. 1:3).

155. I can ever be content for I have Christ (Heb. 13:5).

156. I have all the armor and weapons I need (2 Cor. 10:4; Eph. 6:10-17).

157. I have God's all-sufficient grace (2 Cor. 12:9).

158. I have grace to help in time of need (Heb. 4:16).

159. I have God's power (Eph. 1:19; 3:20).

160. I have access to the Father (Eph. 2:18; Heb. 4:16).

161. I have a great High Priest (Heb. 2:17-18; 3:1; 4:14-16; 8:1; 10:21).

162. I have an unfailing Intercessor (Heb. 7:25; 9:24; Rom. 8:34).

163. I have a righteous Advocate with the Father for times when I sin (1 John 2:1).

164. I have peace with God (Rom. 5:1).

165. Christ is my peace (Eph. 2:14).

166. I have rest for my soul (Matt. 11:28-29; Heb. 4:9).

167. I am led by the Spirit of God (Rom. 8:14).

168. I am enabled during trials and temptations (1 Cor.

10:13).

169. I am given assurance by the Spirit (Rom. 8:16; Heb. 6:18).

170. I am given comfort by God (2 Cor. 1:3-7).

171. I am tranquilized by His peace (Phil. 4:7).

172. I am freely given truth and knowledge by the Spirit (1 Cor. 2:12).

173. I am not distressed (2 Cor. 4:8).

174. I am not in despair (2 Cor. 4:8).

175. I am not forsaken (2 Cor. 4:9).

176. I am not in darkness (1 Thess. 5:4).

177. God is my Sufficiency (2 Cor. 3:5).

178. God is my Strength (2 Cor. 12:9-10; Phil. 4:13).

179. God is my Helper (Heb. 13:6).

180. I belong to a Sovereign God who works all things together for my good (Rom. 8:28).

181. All things are for my sake (2 Cor. 4:15).

182. My God is for me (Rom. 8:31).

183. My every need is supplied (Phil. 4:19).

184. I am a laborer together with Christ (1 Cor. 3:9; 2 Cor. 6:1).

185. I am His workmanship (Eph. 2:10).

186. God works in me (Phil. 2:13; Heb. 13:21).

187. God's Word works in me (1 Thess. 2:13).

188. I am sealed by God (2 Cor. 1:22; Eph. 1:13).

189. I am on the Rock, Christ Jesus (Matt. 16:18; 1 Cor. 3:11).

190. I am established securely in Christ (2 Cor. 1:21; 2 Thess. 3:3).

191. I am kept by the power of God (1 Pet. 1:5).

192. I am preserved in Jesus Christ (Jude 1).

193. I am kept from falling (Jude 24).

194. I have a building of God eternal in the heavens (2 Cor. 5:1).

195. My name is forever written in heaven (Luke 10:20).

196. I am more than a conqueror, even a super-conqueror (Rom. 8:37).

197. I have victory through Christ (1 Cor. 15:57).

198. I have overcome the world (1 John 5:4-5).

199. I always triumph in Christ (2 Cor. 2:14).

200. I am indwelt by the victorious Christ who is greater than Satan (1 John 4:4).

201. Satan cannot touch me (1 John 5:18).

202. I have a living hope (1 Pet. 1:3).

203. I have a glorious future (Rom. 8:18; 2 Thess. 2:14).

204. I have been given eternal encouragement and good hope through grace (2 Thess. 2:16).

205. I will be preserved unto His heavenly kingdom (2 Tim. 4:18).

206. I am receiving a kingdom which cannot be moved (Heb. 12:28).

207. I have a place reserved in heaven for me (John 14:2,3; 1 Pet. 1:4).

208. I will eat of the tree of life (Rev. 2:7).

209. I will not be hurt of the second death (Rev. 2:11; 20:6).

210. I will have a new name (Rev. 2:17; 3:12).

211. I will have power over the nations (Rev. 2:26; 5:10).

212. I will not have my name blotted out of the book of life (Rev. 3:5).

213. I will be a pillar in God's temple (Rev. 3:12).

214. I will sit with Christ in His throne (Rev. 3:21).

215. I will be with my God forever (Rev. 21:3-4).

These spiritual blessings (and many more) are the ____
present____possessions of all believers from the very
moment they believe the Gospel and are placed into an eternal
relationship with Christ by the Holy Spirit (1 Corinthians
12:12-13).

Illustration—Hetty Green is known in American history as
"America's Greatest Miser." Yet, when she died in 1916, she
left an estate valued at $100 million. That was a lot of money
in 1916! It is said that Hetty was so miserly that she ate cold
oatmeal because she thought it was too expensive to heat
the water to warm it. Her son had a severe leg injury, but
because she delayed so long to find a free clinic, his leg had
to be ____**amputated**____. Eventually, she had an attack
of apoplexy (bleeding within internal organs) which hastened
her own death, while arguing over the merits of skim milk
because it was cheaper than whole milk. Though Hetty was
very wealthy, she lived like a beggar because she did not __
understand____ or utilize her financial resources. Will the
same be said spiritually of you in your Christian life? Will you
access by faith your spiritual riches in Christ (Romans 5:2) and
live your life consistent with your position in Christ (Ephesians
4:1)? This is a great reason to begin studying your Bible; for
only in God's Word will you read about your ____**spiritual**____
wealth and assets in Christ.

WHAT NOW?—ETERNAL SECURITY IN CHRIST

INTRODUCTION

It is very clear on a human level that children grow best in a home where they know they are loved unconditionally and are secure in their relationship with their parents. The Bible is equally clear that this same truth is found in the spiritual ___**realm**___. Remember, one did not enter the family of God through behavior, but through ___**birth**___. God wants every born-again believer (i.e. those who have put their faith in Jesus Christ) to know that they are unconditionally loved by Him and that they are eternally secure in their ___**family**___ relationship with God. The assurance of this great scriptural truth is the birthright of every believer in Christ and is based upon the following two things...

The ___Promises___ of God
1. Eternal life lasts ___**forever**___, by definition (John 3:14-16).
2. Sin cannot condemn a believer (John 3:18; John 5:24, Romans 8:1).
3. A believer can never be cast out (John 6:35-37).
4. It is God's will that the believer is never lost (John 6:38-

40).

5. No one can snatch the believer out of _____ **Jesus** 's hand (John 10:27-28).

6. No one can snatch the believer out of the _____ **Father** 's hand (John 10:29).

7. God has pre-determined to glorify the believer all based upon His grace and not the believer's behavior (Romans 8:28-30).

8. No one or nothing can separate the believer from the _____ **love** _____ of God in Christ Jesus (Romans 8:35-39).

9. Salvation is a gift from God and therefore irrevocable (Romans 6:23, Ephesians 2:8-9, Romans 11:29)

10. A believer is _____ **sealed** _____ with the Holy Spirit until the day of redemption (Ephesians 1:13-14).

11. Salvation is a permanent reality that is not obtained or maintained by one's holy life or works (Ephesians 2:8-10).

12. Christ promised never to _____ **leave** _____ or forsake the believer (Hebrews 13:5).

13. The believer is kept by the power of God (1 Peter 1:3-5).

14. God began the good work in us and will _____ **complete** _____ it (Philippians 1:6).

15. God will confirm the believer until the end (1 Corinthians 1:8).

The Work of Christ

1. Christ was well pleasing to the Father during His **life** _____ (Matthew 3:17, Mark 1:11, Luke 3:22, Matthew 12:18, Matthew 17:5), and also at His **death** _____ (Romans 3:25, 1 John 2:2, 1 John 4:10).

2. The believer is perfected forever because of Christ's

finished work on the cross (Hebrews 10:10-14).

3. Christ's work on the cross ensures that no one can indict the believer in the __**future**__ or condemn the believer in the _____**present**_____ (Romans 8:31-34, 1 John 2:1-2).

4. Christ plans on presenting the church without spot or wrinkle...holy, without blemish (Ephesians 5:25-27).

5. Christ's present work is to make _____**intercession**_____ for the believer (Hebrews 7:25), and He also functions as the believer's _____**advocate**_____ (i.e. attorney) when the believer does sin (1 John 2:1-2).

Illustration

No matter how hard one might try, they could never un-do their own physical birth into their earthly family. It is a once-for-all occurrence that can never be repeated or undone. The same is true with the believer's spiritual birth. It is a once-for-all, non-repeatable birth that cannot be undone since it is fully accomplished by __**God**__. But *entering the family of God* at a moment in time when you trust in Christ as Savior must be kept distinct from the believer's *daily fellowship with God.* Entering the family of God happens at a point in time when you put your __**faith**__ in Jesus Christ and His work for you, and everything from that point forward involves your daily fellowship with God, commonly referred to as your "walk with God" or "living the Christian life." Let's be clear...God does not ask a non-Christian to "live the Christian life" in order to get to heaven, **NOR** does God ask a Christian to "live the Christian life" to make sure he or she is _____**worthy**_____ to get to heaven. God desires the believer in Jesus Christ to "live the Christian life" because this is how God has designed and wired the believer to live (Ephesians 2:10), and because a believer who walks by faith and dependence upon the Lord through their daily lives bring great glory and honor to Him.

What Happens When the Believer Sins?

Sin in the life of the child of God breaks ___ **fellowship** ___ with God (1 John 1:3-7) and displeases Him. Sin also brings God's loving discipline upon that believer (Hebrews 12:5-11) if he or she refuses to acknowledge and confess his or her sin (1 John 1:9-10). Nevertheless, the believer ___ **remains** ___ a child of God because Jesus Christ already paid for all our sins. Yet personal sin affects the believer's *daily fellowship with God.*

If you are a parent, you can certainly relate to these scriptural principles of "family" VS. "fellowship." From the first day of their birth to the present, your children have been and will always be part of your ___ **family** ___. They have your DNA. They will always be your children whether they obey you or rebel against you. Why? It is because they have been birthed by you. Yet, when your children have rebelled against your will and direction for them, you have become displeased with them—the fellowship has been broken until some admission occurs. (See chart below).

In the same way, every child of God has been born again at the moment they accepted the Gospel by faith. They now have the DNA of God. They have been spiritually birthed by God Himself, and they are children of God regardless of their daily behavior or performance. However, when believers choose to sin and disobey their Heavenly Father, they break fellowship with Him. This also displeases the Lord. But they remain a _____**child**_____ of God in the family of God. Why? It is because they have been "born again" by God Himself.[1]

FAMILY OF GOD *vs.* FELLOWSHIP WITH GOD

...truly our fellowship is with the Father and with His Son Jesus Christ. And these things we write to you that your joy may be full.   I JOHN 1:3-4

There is only one way to be born again - by faith in Jesus Christ alone.

FAMILY OF GOD

FELLOWSHIP WITH GOD

SIN

CONFESS

JOY

MISERY

Faith

SINS

LOST SINNER

For you are all sons of God through faith in Christ Jesus
GALATIANS 3:26

If we confess our sins, He is faithful and just to forgive us our sins and to cleanse us from all unrighteousness.   I JOHN 1:9

WHAT NOW?—HOW TO COMMUNICATE WITH GOD

INTRODUCTION

As a new believer in Jesus Christ it is vital that you remember that true biblical Christianity is not a religion of human achievement, but rather a **relationship** with God of divine accomplishment. As a result of being born again, God wants the believer to grow in their relationship with Him and enjoy sweet fellowship with Him on a daily basis. Much like a healthy parent-child relationship, both sides want the relationship to be a close one. But how does one grow in their relationship with God? This study will examine the way believers **communicate** with God.

God communicates with us through His Word

1 Peter 2:2 tells us, "As newborn babes, desire the pure milk of the word, that you may grow thereby." Just as a newborn baby has a great longing for his or her mother's milk, so believers are to intensely choose to desire the milk of God's **Word** to grow spiritually. This is how God communicates to His children. God speaks to you today not in visions, dreams,

or ecstatic experiences, but through the reading, study, and memorization of God's Word. Jesus Christ stated emphatically in Matthew 4:4, "It is written, 'Man shall not live by bread alone, but by every word that proceeds from the mouth of God.'" God wants you to ___**know**___ Him, and He has chosen to reveal Himself to us through His written Word. In addition, God will use His Word to transform you internally to become more and more like Jesus Christ. 2 Corinthians 3:18 says, "But we all, with unveiled face, beholding as in a mirror the glory of the Lord, are being transformed into the same image from glory to glory, just as by the Spirit of the Lord." Additionally, God will use His word to instruct you and ___**prepare**___ or equip you for your life ahead as 2 Timothy 3:16-17 says, "All Scripture is given by inspiration of God, and is profitable for doctrine, for reproof, for correction, for instruction in righteousness, that the man of God may be complete, thoroughly equipped for every good work." The Word of God is ___**vital**___ to your communication with God and to your spiritual growth.

Read the Bible on your ___*Own*___

Like any good human relationship, the more time you invest in getting to know the other person, the better the relationship will be. Having a relationship with God is no different, and thus spending time ___**reading**___ and studying the Bible on your own will be time well spent in growing in your relationship with God. The indwelling Holy Spirit desires to lead you to a correct understanding of the Word of God as we depend upon Him to do so.

Listen to the Bible taught by gifted men

Ephesians 4:11-12 tells us, "And He Himself gave some to be

apostles, some prophets, some evangelists, and some pastors and teachers, for the equipping of the saints for the work of ministry, for the edifying of the body of Christ." We learn elsewhere in Ephesians that the office of apostles and prophets were used to lay the **foundation** of the church in the 1st century, but the offices of evangelist, and pastor-teacher still exist in our day. These men are not "super-saints," but rather hold a unique office and gifting in the church. They are **tools** used by God in the lives of all saints to teach them the Word of God and to equip them for service. Related to your growing in your relationship with God, this is a **practical** way God increases your understanding of Him.

The believer communicates with God through prayer

Communication, by definition, requires at least **two** parties. We have looked at the way God communicates with us, but we have yet to look at how we communicate with God. The Bible tells us that we communicate with God through **prayer**. In fact, God has given His children the privilege to pray to Him in praise, thanksgiving, admission, or confession of sin (for fellowship with God), communicating our struggles, and making requests for others and for our own needs. But what exactly is prayer? Simply put, prayer is **talking** to God. You do not have to be a pastor or seminary-trained person to pray to God...you can talk to Him just as you are.

How often should I pray

The Bible gives some clear teaching in this manner, but before we look at the Scriptures let's ask ourselves a question using a human illustration. How often should I talk to my ____

friend_____ if I want to grow in my relationship with them? Clearly the answer would be "often," "a lot," "consistently," etc. The answer to "how often should I pray?" would be answered much the same way. In fact the Bible says in Philippians 4:6, "Be anxious for nothing, but in **_everything_** by prayer and supplication, with thanksgiving, let your requests be made known to God." Elsewhere in 1 Thessalonians 5:17, Paul simply states, "Pray without **_ceasing_**." Very clearly, the Bible (God communicating with us) would encourage us to speak with God and take advantage of that privilege ___**every**___ chance we can. The fringe benefits of doing so are overwhelming…not only do we grow in our relationship with God, but notice what God provides when we speak with him, "and the ___**peace**___ of God, which surpasses all understanding, will guard your hearts and minds through Christ Jesus," (Philippians 4:7).

If God knows everything already, why should I pray?
The answer seems to rest in the idea that prayer conveys an attitude of total ___**dependence**___ on God to meet our every need. Every prayer you express is a demonstration of faith (or dependence) on God to meet your needs physically, spiritually, emotionally, and mentally. Also, it is important to remember that while God is sovereign (i.e. He is in complete control), yet He amazingly factors our prayers into His ___**plans**___ and will for us. Thus, we should ask the Lord in faith to consider our petitions and to act according to His will.

CONCLUSION
Remember, you do not get close to God overnight. It is developed day by day, week by week, and month by month as you take time talking with Him and allowing Him to speak to

you through His Word, the Bible. The more you spend time with Him, the more you will discover that Christianity is not a matter of following a __**list**__ of rules, rituals, and regulations. It is a growing, dynamic relationship with Jesus Christ. Like everything in the Christian life, if you are willing God will use His Word to mature you by His grace when it comes to learning how to ____**pray**__ effectively, just like your communication skills increased as you grew from childhood to adulthood.

WHAT NOW?—SPIRITUAL GIFTS
AND THE LOCAL CHURCH

INTRODUCTION

It is clear from the Scriptures that God did not intend believers in Jesus Christ to navigate life as "Lone Ranger" Christians. That is, God has developed in His plan to include you and I in an **organic** group called the "church." The Greek word used to translate the word church simply means "called out ones," and thus the church is comprised of people who are called out from the world and are called to a relationship with Jesus Christ through faith in Him and His finished work. The church is **NOT** a building, but rather buildings are where the church (i.e. believers in Jesus Christ) **meets**. Why is the local church so important and so vital to a believer's spiritual growth? Let us consider the following reasons...

We were baptized into the body of Christ

1 Corinthians 12:13 says, "For by one Spirit we were **all** baptized into one body—whether Jews or Greeks, whether slaves or free—and have **all** been made to drink into one Spirit." This spiritual baptism, not involving **water**, was performed at a point in time when you and I put our

faith in Jesus Christ and it has ALREADY HAPPENED to you and was accomplished by the Holy Spirit of God. Whether we realize it or not, you and I have been joined to the body of Christ, and we are members of His body, of which Jesus Christ is the head. Much like our human bodies, different parts of the body have different functions, and many of them are inter-related and dependent upon another body part to do their function well. Truly, "the ankle bone is connected to the shin bone, the shin bone is connected to the knee bone, and so on…" When the human body has body parts not doing their **function** , we call that "disease" and it usually results in sickness or health issues. The same can be said of the body of Christ if believers are not engaged, involved, and seeking to perform their **needed** function for the benefit of everyone else in the body.

God has uniquely placed you in the body for a reason and your contribution is needed and important

Ephesians 4:11-13 told us of God's plan for believers to be taught the Word of God by gifted men given to the church for the express purpose of equipping believers for the work of the ministry. Further on in that passage (verses 15-16) Paul says this regarding the believer's place in the body of Christ, "But, speaking the truth in love, may grow up in all things into Him who is the head—Christ—From whom the whole body, joined and knit together by what *every joint supplies*, according to the effective working by which *every part does its share*, causes growth of the body for the edifying of itself in love." Whether you are the pastor of a church, or the person who simply makes the coffee each Sunday morning in an act of **service** , you are a much-needed part in the body of Christ. In fact, every believer is needed to build up (i.e. edify) the church and to cause spiritual __**growth**__ in others. Bottom line is that God's desire is that each individual member of the body of Christ fulfill their own God-ordained and God-equipped role in dependence upon Him for the carrying out of the tasks assigned. This is true __**health**__ in a church situation.

Your __**physical**__ *presence with other believers is desired by God*

For many, including Christians, Sunday is an extra day, like Saturday, to sleep in. After all, most of us have the Monday-Friday 8am to 5pm grind to deal with, and so why wake up early one more day a week? This is __**worldly**__ wisdom (see James 3:14-15 for its source) and is contrary to the way God views the situation. In fact, we get God's insight on the situation in Hebrews 10:24-25 as other believers during Bible times apparently struggled with the same concept of getting together, "And let us consider one another in order to stir up love and good works, ***not forsaking the assembling of ourselves together***, as is the manner of some, but exhorting one another, and so much the more as you see the Day approaching." Notice, that one of the benefits of gathering with other believers is that you provide a sort of "positive __**peer**__ pressure," if you will, to continue to spur each other on to love and good works. Additionally, there is positive exhortation that comes from being around other like-minded believers, and you can encourage one another in the __**Lord**__.

The gathering together of believers is the place where pastor-teachers teach the Word of God

Local church gatherings are the appointed time each week

where the gifted men of Ephesians 4:11-13 teach the Word of God which is designed to equip you to function and __ **fulfill**_____ God's ministry for your life. It is imperative that believers place a high value on that appointed time and adjust their _____**schedule**_____ accordingly to be there. If God has put all of this into place as the means by which He desires your spiritual growth, others' spiritual growth, and the fulfillment of your mission and purpose, how could we not _____**value**_____ this time accordingly?

Your valuable role in the church is a result of your new spiritual gifting

Every believer in Jesus Christ has been gifted spiritually to function within the body, and in ministry to an unsaved world to cause the body to grow spiritually. Notice how 1 Corinthians 12:4-7 words it, "There are diversities of gifts, but the same Spirit. There are differences of ministries, but the same Lord. And there are diversities of activities, but it is the same God who works all in all. But the manifestation of the Spirit is given to *each one* for the profit *of all.*" Everyone is differently and uniquely gifted, and yet each one is needed for the _____**profit**_____ of all believers. The list of spiritual gifts found in the New Testament are: Teachers, Pastors, Evangelism, Ministering/Service, Faith, Exhortation/Encouragement, Discernment, Showing Mercy, Giving, and Administration. Others mentioned, but whose use has since ceased with the apostolic era are: Apostleship, Prophecy, Miracles/Healings, and Speaking in New Languages (Tongues). It is O.K. and desirable for one to seek to know their own spiritual gifting, but the best way to accomplish that is to fellowship with the __**saints**__, learn the _____**Word**_____of God, believe what you read, and walk by faith in dependence upon the Lord in your **daily** life. Your gifting should become evident as you serve others and grow in your relationship with the Lord.

CONCLUSION

The Bible is clear, going to church on Sunday mornings is not about ruining what would be a perfectly good day to **sleep** **in** a little more, and get some extra things done around the house before you go back to work on Monday. God Himself designed the local body of believers to function together with each individual part designed and placed into the body by God to serve its **function** within the body. Jesus says in Matthew 16:18, "…I will build my church…" Since God takes great **value** in the local church, should we not do the same?

WHAT NOW?—SECOND COMING OF CHRIST

INTRODUCTION

Since God has promised the believer everlasting life the very moment he or she believes in Christ as Savior (John 3:16), the believer never needs to fear **death** again as they may have before they were saved. In fact, the Bible says this about the believer who dies, "So *we are* always confident, knowing that while we are at home in the body we are absent from the Lord. For we walk by faith, not by sight. We are confident, yes, well pleased rather to be ***absent from the body and to be present with the Lord***" (2 Corinthians 5:6-8). The moment the believer's soul and spirit become absent or separated from the body at physical death, he or she will be **present** with the Lord. There is no such thing in the Bible as "soul sleep" upon death, though your body will "sleep" in a figurative sense in the grave awaiting the day that it is resurrected and reunited with your redeemed soul.

Some believers will not **physically** *die*

One of the most incredible teachings of Scripture is that the believer does not *have to* physically die. The Scriptures clearly teach that one generation of Christians will not **die** but

39

will be **raptured** alive to meet Jesus Christ in the clouds and return directly to heaven with Him. 1 Thessalonians 4:16-18 says, "For the Lord Himself will descend from heaven with a shout, with the voice of an archangel, and with the trumpet of God. And the dead in Christ will rise first. Then we who are alive *and* remain shall be caught up together with them in the clouds to meet the Lord in the air. And thus we shall always be with the Lord. Therefore comfort one another with these words." 1 Corinthians 15:51-53 says, "Behold, I tell you a mystery: We shall not all sleep, but we shall all be changed—in a moment, in the twinkling of an eye, at the last trumpet. For the trumpet will sound, and the dead will be raised incorruptible, and we shall be changed. For this corruptible must put on incorruption, and this mortal *must* put on immortality." From these two verses we learn the following things regarding the rapture of the church: (1) __**All**__ believers alive at the time of the rapture will be raptured (**NOT** just the "super-spiritual"), (2) The rapture happens with an announcement of some sort and happens very __**quickly**__, (3) This is the point in time that the living believer gets their glorified __**body**__, and (4) Those believers who have died from the time of the Day of Pentecost (Acts 2) till the day of the rapture will have their bodies resurrected in an immortal state and they will be rejoined with their souls and spirits, which have been with the Lord in His presence since their __**death**__.

All believers will be rewarded for the way they lived their lives on earth

Immediately following the rapture of the church, and the resurrection of the dead saints in Christ, the entire church will appear before the __**Bema**__ Seat Judgment of Christ.

2 Corinthians 5:10 says, "For we must all appear before the judgment seat of Christ, that each one may receive the things done in the body, according to what he has done, whether good or bad." Notice clearly that **ALL** believers will appear before this reward judgment seat. 1 Corinthians 3:11-15 gives us a good idea on exactly what Jesus Christ will be judging on this day, "For no other foundation can anyone lay than that which is laid, which is Jesus Christ. Now if anyone builds on this foundation *with* gold, silver, precious stones, wood, hay, straw, each one's work will become clear; for the Day will declare it, because it will be revealed by fire; and the fire will test each one's work, of what sort it is. If anyone's work which he has built on *it* endures, he will receive a reward. If anyone's work is burned, he will suffer loss; but he himself will be saved, yet so as through fire." The constant message for the believer in Jesus Christ is that God saves us by His grace, and that He also enables us to live a life that would bring Him glory also by and through His grace. Each believer will be held _____**accountable**_____ for the way they responded to the Word of God in their lives in terms of the good __**works**__ they do in dependence upon the Lord, thus acceptable/rewardable (Ephesians 2:10).

Jesus Christ is coming back
We have already discussed Jesus Christ's coming in the clouds to call living believers to Himself at the rapture. Following the rapture, the world will undergo a seven-year time period known in the Scriptures as the Great ____**Tribulation**____ period. This time period will begin when a world leader, later identified as the antichrist will sign a ____**seven**____ -year covenant with the nation of Israel, and it will be a time in which God pours out His wrath upon the earth. This time period is described

in Revelation 6-19, and it is going to be the worst and most difficult seven years in human ___**history**___! Following these seven years, Jesus Christ Himself will come back to earth with the church-aged believers (Revelation 19:11-21) to establish an earthly ___**Kingdom**___ where He will reign over Israel and all other nations from His physical throne in Jerusalem. All church-aged believers and all Old Testament believers will reign with Christ in His kingdom and serve in some sort of administration function with Christ. This kingdom will last 1,000 years (Revelation 20:1-10) and it will conclude with the final judgment of Satan as well as the bodily resurrection and final judgment of all unbelievers from the beginning of history at the Great ___**White**___ Throne Judgment (Revelation 20:11-15). Following this judgment, the current earth and current heaven will be destroyed by ___**fire**___ (2 Peter 3:10-13), and God will create a new heaven and a new earth which will include a new city called the "New Jerusalem" (described in Revelation 21-22). This will be the home of every believer for ___**eternity**___.

What is your proper response to Jesus Christ's coming

The Scriptures are clear what the coming of Jesus Christ should do ___**mentally**___ for the believer in terms of living their daily lives. 2 Peter 3:11-14 says, "Therefore, since all these things will be dissolved, what manner *of persons* ought you to be in holy conduct and godliness, looking for and hastening the coming of the day of God, because of which the heavens will be dissolved, being on fire, and the elements will melt with fervent heat? Nevertheless we, according to His promise, look for new heavens and a new earth in which righteousness dwells. Therefore, beloved, looking forward to these things, be diligent to be found by Him in peace, without spot and blameless." God would have the believer's motivation as one who is ready and eagerly ____**anticipating**____ the Lord's return. Because of this desire to be ready in anticipation of the Lord's return, the believer wants to be about the Lord's work and to be found in this manner when the Lord returns. No believer wants to be ____**ashamed**____ at His coming, because maybe they are involved in sin, or living a life of selfish indifference towards spiritual things.

CONCLUSION

The Bible contains good news that Jesus Christ is coming again. One reason we know that He will come again physically and ____**literally**____ is because of what the angels said to His disciples when He ascended, "Now when He had spoken these things, while they watched, He was taken up, and a cloud received Him out of their sight. And while they looked steadfastly toward heaven as He went up, behold, two men stood by them in white apparel, who also said, 'Men of Galilee, why do you stand gazing up into heaven? This *same* Jesus, who was taken up from you into heaven, will so come *in like manner* as you saw Him go into heaven.'" The truth of Christ's coming in the clouds for His church at the rapture should ____**motivate**____ and stimulate the believer towards living a godly life by depending upon the Spirit of God in all of his or her good works.

WHAT NOW?—SPIRITUAL GROWTH: THE THREE TENSES OF SALVATION

INTRODUCTION

While spiritual birth must precede spiritual growth, God now wants you to ___**grow**___ in grace and become more and more like His Son, Jesus Christ. This is what spiritual growth is all about. Just getting a ticket punched for your final destination (i.e. heaven) is not all there is to God's message of salvation. The Bible describes a "full" plan of salvation, and it is found in three different phases or _____**tenses**___. Remember, you are forever and eternally saved the moment you put your faith in Jesus Christ and His finished work on the cross and His resurrection. But this is merely the first stage or first phase or tense of salvation. Looking at ___**all**___ the phases or tenses of our ONE wonderful salvation is what this study is about.

1st Tense of Salvation: ____**Justification**____

In each tense of salvation, it is beneficial to start the conversation with a question..."Salvation from ___**what**___?" In the first phase of salvation, the answer to that question is that we *have*

45

been (past tense) saved from the **_penalty_** of sin when we put our faith in Jesus Christ and His finished work on the cross and His resurrection. Romans 6:23 describes this penalty when it says, "For the wages of sin *is* death, but the gift of God *is* eternal life in Christ Jesus our Lord." At the exact moment we transfer our faith to Jesus Christ, God justifies us, or He *declares* us _____**righteous**_____. Romans 5:1 says, "Therefore, having been *justified* by faith, we have peace with God through our Lord Jesus Christ." Romans 4:5 says, "But to him who does not work but believes on Him who *justifies* the ungodly, his faith is accounted for righteousness." This one time moment of _____**faith**_____ in Jesus Christ results in many things: our spiritual birth, our eternal destiny being changed from hell that we deserved to a heaven we do not, our position IN Christ, possessors of every spiritual blessing and a guaranteed inheritance in heaven.

2nd Tense of Salvation: Sanctification

This is the tense of salvation that we live in every day for the rest of our natural lives. "What are we _____**saved**_____ from in this tense?" The answer to that question is that we are *being saved* (present tense) from the **_power_** of sin. Romans 6:1-2 describes the believer's potential to live their lives completely _____**dominated**_____ by the power of the sin nature, "What shall we say then? Shall we continue in sin that grace may abound? Certainly not! How shall we who died to sin live any longer in it?" God has also made provision for the believer to live life in such a way that they are saved/delivered from the sin nature's power in their _____**daily**_____ lives. This tense is called sanctification, literally meaning "to set apart" for God's purposes and use. Romans 6:6 and 6:11 says this, "Knowing this, that our old man was crucified with *Him*, that the body of sin might be done away with, that we should no longer be slaves of sin…Likewise you also, reckon yourselves to be dead indeed to sin, but alive to God in Christ Jesus our Lord." In the first tense we put our faith in Christ and His finished work at a moment in ___**time**___, whereas in the second tense we are to *continue* to put our ___**faith**___ (i.e. V11 "reckon") in God's work in identifying us with Jesus' death, burial, and resurrection. According to Romans 6:6, this is the ONLY way that the body of sin might be done away with OR "rendered inoperative" in our lives. Notice we are justified by grace through a one-time moment of faith, and we are also sanctified by grace through faith, but it is a ___**continual**___ or moment by moment faith. Galatians 5:16 calls this "walking in the Spirit" when it says, "I say then: Walk in the Spirit, and you shall not fulfill the lust of the flesh." The flesh here is synonymous with the "sin nature" and because of the double Greek negation this is saying very strongly that if you walk in the ___**Spirit**___, you will never, ever fulfill the lust of the flesh.

3rd Tense of Salvation: Glorification

This third tense of salvation is still future, but it is guaranteed. Again, "What are we saved from in this third tense?" The answer is that we *will be* saved (future tense) from the very ___**presence**___ of sin. Romans 8:30 speaks of this being a guaranteed result for one who has put their faith in Christ and His finished work at a ___**point**___ in time, "Moreover whom He predestined, these He also called; whom He called, these He also justified; and whom He justified, these He also glorified." Notice that the same group who is justified (i.e. declared righteous/1st tense) is the ___**same**___ group who *will*

be glorified. This glorification takes place either at the believer's
_____**rapture**_____ or at the believer's physical death. Romans
5:9-10 says, "Much more then, having now been justified by
His blood, we *shall be* saved from wrath through Him. For if
when we were enemies we were reconciled to God through the
death of His Son, much more, having been reconciled, we *shall
be* saved by His life."

Where the rubber meets the road

If we as believers live in time and space, then the one tense of
our salvation that is a daily ____**concern**____ is the second tense
(sanctification) deliverance from the power of sin. This is our
daily responsibility, and it impacts our _____**fellowship**_____
with the Lord and spiritual growth in grace. So, the question
becomes, "How do you grow spiritually?" Or even, "How can
we walk more consistently to grow in our sanctification and/
or have more victory over the sin nature in our daily life?"
These are the million-dollar questions that we face as we go
to ____**work**____, drive our cars, fill up the gas, pay the bills,
interact with our employer, deal with family issues, etc. From
Romans 6, we learn that we must first *KNOW* what God has
done to make provision for victory over the sin nature, and
once we *KNOW* we should COUNT ON what God has done
by ____**faith**____, and then as we continue to COUNT ON God's
provision by faith, we then PRESENT our physical bodies to
God as instruments of righteousness. In other words, God
wants to accomplish righteous acts that bring Him honor
and glory through your bodies. He only does this in the
believer who KNOWS God's provision, COUNTS ON God's
provision, and PRESENTS his body to God based upon God's
____**provision**____. That begs the question, "What exactly is

God's provision?" God crucified us with Christ, buried us with Christ, and resurrected us with Christ to newness of life. In our identification with Jesus Christ, our relationship to the sin nature has been ____**severed**____, and for the first time in our lives we do not have to be slaves to sin unless we choose to yield ourselves to it and its desires. When we do this then ____**individual**____ sins manifest themselves in our lives (See Galatians 5:19-21). However, when we KNOW, COUNT ON, and PRESENT we manifest fruit that is acceptable to God (See Galatians 5:22-23).

CONCLUSION (See chart below).[1]

<u>Three Tenses of Salvation</u>

Tense or Phase	1st	2nd	3rd
Time Element	*Past*	*Present*	*Future*
Saved From What	PENALTY of sin (in Hell)	POWER of sin (in your daily life)	PRESENCE of sin (in heaven)
Scripture	John 3:17; 1 Corinthians 1:21; Titus 3:5; Ephesians 2:8-9	1 Corinthians 1:17-18; 15:1-2; 1Philippians 2:12-13; 1 Timothy 4:16; James 1:21; 5:20	Romans 5:9; 13:11; 1 Corinthians 3:15
Theological Terminology	JUSTIFICATION	SANCTIFICATION	GLORIFICATION
Time Factor	Point in Time (A one-time moment of faith)	Process of Time (Repeated responses of faith)	Point of Time (A one-time moment of faith – SAME MOMENT as justification)
Condition(s)	By God's grace alone through faith alone in Christ alone (Acts 16:30-31)	By God's grace alone through yielded and daily dependence on the Lord via the Holy Spirit (Romans 6:1-14; 8:1-4)	By death (2 Corinthians 5:10) or by Rapture (1 Thessalonians 4:13-18)

All three tenses of salvation in one passage: "For the grace of God that brings salvation *has appeared to all men* (1st Tense), teaching us that, *denying ungodliness and worldly lusts, we should live soberly, righteously, and godly in the present age* (2nd Tense), *looking for the blessed hope and glorious appearing of our great God and Savior Jesus Christ* (3rd Tense)," – Titus 2:11-13

WHAT NOW?—SPIRITUAL GROWTH: GOD'S GRACE DESIGN FOR IT

INTRODUCTION

Spiritual birth should result in spiritual ___**growth**___ as the believer progresses from Christian babyhood, to spiritual adolescence, to becoming a mature believer in the faith (1 John 2:13-14). While there is nothing wrong with being a babe in Christ (since we all began there!), there is definitely something wrong if you ___**remain**___ a babe in your growth or later retrogress back into spiritual immaturity after you have grown in your knowledge of God's Word. 1 Corinthians 3:1-3 says, "And I, brethren, could not speak to you as to spiritual *people* but as to carnal, as to babes in Christ. I fed you with milk and not with solid food; for until now you were not able to *receive it*, and even now you are still not able; for you are still carnal. For where *there are* envy, strife, and divisions among you, are you not carnal and behaving like *mere* men?" Like with your salvation from sin's penalty, God has provided everything necessary by His grace for you to grow as a child of God, except for the faith that you must learn to ___**exercise**___ in daily dependence upon Him and His promises. So, what is involved in God's grace-design for your spiritual growth?

Spiritual growth takes time

While spiritual birth takes a moment of time where a person puts his or her faith in the finished work of Jesus Christ, spiritual growth and maturity do not occur ____**overnight**____; it takes time. 2 Peter 3:18 says, "But grow in the grace and knowledge of our Lord and Savior Jesus Christ." Growth, by definition, takes time and implies a gradual ____**process**____. We need to be patient when it comes to our spiritual growth. God is not in a hurry and we certainly do not need to be either. Remember that when God wants to produce a squash, He takes six months. But when God wants to produce a solid oak tree, He takes a hundred ____**years**____. Which one do you want to be? God wants to make adjustments in your ____**thinking**____, your motives, your relationships, but He does so graciously and patiently, in love, over time.

Spiritual growth takes truth

The great need of your Christian life is not to do "great things for God." Instead it is to get firmly ____**established**____ in the Word of God through the personal reading and public teaching of the Scriptures. Remember, God has placed pastor-teachers in your life to expound and exegete the Scriptures to equip you for the work of the ____**ministry**____. 2 Timothy 2:15 says, "Be diligent to present yourself approved to God, a worker who does not need to be ashamed, rightly dividing the word of truth," and 2 Timothy 3:16-17 says, "All Scripture *is* given by inspiration of God, and is profitable for doctrine, for reproof, for correction, for instruction in righteousness, that the man of God may be complete, thoroughly equipped for every good work." Much like a baby must take in both milk and meat to grow, so the new believer must feed on the milk and meat of the Word of __**God**__ to grow.

Spiritual growth requires sound TEACHERS

To facilitate your growth, God has given you a permanent and _____**indwelling**_____ teacher, the Holy Spirit. The Holy Spirit is to be your ultimate teacher and it is He who illuminates God's Word and His truth for us. 1 Corinthians 2:12, "Now we have received, not the spirit of the world, but the Spirit who is from God, that we might know the things that have been freely given to us by God." In addition to the ultimate teacher, God has also provided _____**human**_____ teachers as grace-gifts to the Church (See Ephesians 4:11-16). Unfortunately, in our day, many churches are more focused on 'entertaining the goats' instead of 'feeding the sheep.' Some churches have replaced an emphasis on sound Bible teaching with an emphasis on musical performances, programs, and other forms of _____**entertainment**_____. It is the Word of God, and the Word of God alone which will meet people's __**real**__ spiritual needs, and hence God desires each one of us to put ourselves under and listen to sound Bible teaching in order to grow spiritually.

Spiritual growth requires TRIALS

What is a trial? A trial is anything that __**tests**__ your faith or confidence in God. The Bible describes various types of trials that Christians will encounter. Contrary to popular teachers in Christendom today, the believer is _____**called**_____ to a life of trials and suffering. 2 Peter 2:20-21 says, "For what credit *is it* if, when you are beaten for your faults, you take it patiently?

But when you do good and suffer, if you take it patiently, this *is* commendable before God. For to this **you were called**, because Christ also suffered for us, leaving us an example, that you should follow His steps." Why would God allow trials if they are difficult and cause us to suffer? The Bible teaches that God has a _____**purpose**_____ in allowing trials or "tests." Much like a student in school when they are taught information, the teacher then tests their knowledge of what they learned. So, tests or trials for believers give them an opportunity to ___**apply**___ God's Word. Trials are designed to help the believer in Jesus Christ. James 1:2-4 says, "My brethren, count it all joy when you fall into various trials, knowing that the testing of your faith produces patience. But let patience have *its* perfect work, that you may be perfect and complete, lacking nothing." It is only as you know and understand God's purposes for trials that you can accept them and trust Him for it.

Spiritual growth requires TRUST
Faith is the only response that ___**pleases**___ God. Any other response involves human wisdom or human good, and those emanate from the sin nature and do not give God the glory. To be able to trust God despite "circumstances," despite "other people," despite the "wisdom of our day," is commendable in God's eyes. Hebrews 11:6 says, "But without faith *it is* impossible to please *Him*, for he who comes to God must believe that He is, and *that* He is a rewarder of those who diligently seek Him." God longs for His children to simply trust Him and allow Him to **lead** them by the hand. By believing God's Word and resting by faith in His promises to us amidst the trials and tribulations of life, the believer will effectively ___**grow**___ spiritually.

CONCLUSION

Spiritual growth is the __**work**__ of God accomplished through the preaching of the Word, the trials of life, and through the prayer of the saints.[1] Are you willing to let God bring you through the process of spiritual growth stage-by-stage to make you more and more like His Son? You will be glad that you did! 2 Corinthians 3:18 says, "But we all, with unveiled face, beholding as in a mirror the glory of the Lord, are being transformed into the __**same**__ image from glory to glory, just as by the Spirit of the Lord."

ENDNOTES

Chapter 1:
1. The Hebrew word translated "filthy rags" actually speaks of womens' menstrual rags.

Chapter 2:
1. http://www.middletownbiblechurch.org/salvatio/215thing.htm

Chapter 3:
1. The Family of God vs. Fellowship With God chart was first taught to me by the elders of Duluth Bible Church in Duluth, MN. I made some minor graphic changes to the diagram in an effort to explain the concepts with additional visual helps.

Chapter 7:
1. The 3 Tenses of Salvation chart was first taught to me by the elders of Duluth Bible Church in Duluth, MN. I made some minor changes to the chart for my own teaching ministry.

Chapter 8:
1. Commentary on 2 Thessalonians by J. Hampton Keathley III. (https://bible.org/series/2-thessalonians-exegetical-and-devotional-commentary).

ABOUT THE AUTHOR

Dr. John Thomas Clark holds his bachelor's degree in Mathematics from the University of Texas at San Antonio, has a master's degree in Theology (Th.M.) from Tyndale Theological Seminary and Biblical Institute, and his doctorate degree (DMin) with an emphasis on expository preaching from Dallas Theological Seminary. He values systematic, verse-by-verse Bible teaching and enjoys drawing out truths from the original languages. John has served as the Senior Pastor of Grace Community Fellowship in Newnan, Georgia since September 2016. Additionally, John is a founding board member of DM2 (Disciple Makers Multiplied), a mission organization focused on pastoral training and discipleship of other disciple-makers. John leads DM2's field to Liberia, Africa and travels there twice a year to train pastors. John's first and foremost ministry lies in being a husband to his wife, Carrie, and a loving father to their five children. For more teaching from Pastor John Clark, please visit www.gracenewnan.org

www.ingramcontent.com/pod-product-compliance
Lightning Source LLC
Chambersburg PA
CBHW070800050426
42452CB00012B/2425